G O L F

A game in which one hits a small, hard ball

with special clubs on an outdoor course,

attempting to use as few strokes as

possible to get the ball into a hole.

T I G E R

A wild animal that is usually not found

on golf courses. That is, unless he is able

to shoot in lower numbers than most,

if not all, of his opponents.

This isn't a story about golf. It's a story about a mixed-race kid from California who made up his mind to grow up to be the best golfer in the world. His name is Tiger Woods. (Well, his first name is really Eldrick, but nobody—not even his parents—ever calls him that.) He was born on December 30, 1976, in California.

When Tiger was just a baby, less than one year old, he used to play in the family's garage, hitting golf balls with a sawed-off golf club. His dad, Earl Woods, a retired lieutenant colonel, had only been playing golf for a couple of years himself, but he saw that the little boy really seemed to enjoy it. He began to take little Tiger to the Navy Golf Course, which was just a five-minute drive from their house in Cypress, California.

His mother, Kultida (Tida), used to take Tiger to a **driving range** when he was only eighteen months old. A driving range is a place where people can get a bucketful of golf balls and practice hitting the balls as hard and straight as they can. This helps them improve their **drive**, the long, first hit of each hole, also called **teeing off**.

"When he was done hitting, I would put him back in the stroller and he'd fall asleep," she says. When the other little kids were playing in sandboxes, Tiger practiced hitting golfballs out of **sand traps**.

"I want to be the Michael Jordan of golf," Tiger says about his ambition to be the best he can be. Tiger likes basketball, too. When he was in high school, he played guard. He also tried several other sports. He was good at all of them! In baseball he was a "switch hitter," able to hit equally well with either hand. In track, he was a 400-meter runner. He played wide receiver in football. But he quit all of them because they interfered with his golf, because he has always loved golf most of all.

When Tiger was just three years old, he

was already so good at the game that he was featured on a national TV show called *The Mike Douglas Show*. People could hardly believe that the tiny boy could swing a club and hit a ball with such accuracy.

But back at the Navy Golf Course, somebody had looked up an old rule that said that children under ten years old couldn't play there. Tiger was disappointed. His dad was angry. Earl Woods thought that the rule had been applied to his son because Tiger was part African-American. There were other children under ten playing on the course, but they were all white kids.

When a new golf pro arrived the next year, Tiger's dad bet the man that if he "spotted" the boy one stroke for each hole, Tiger could win. "Give my son a one-stroke handicap for each of nine holes," he said, "and if he wins, he gets playing privileges." The pro agreed and Tiger won!

His talent on the golf course attracted so much attention that he was featured on another television show, *That's Incredible!* And Tiger really was incredible! Imagine a four-year-old skinny little kid regularly playing golf with grown ups—and usually winning!

But before long someone else decided to enforce that old rule and—once again—Tiger was banned from the course. This time Tiger and his dad decided to play at another course in nearby Long Beach.

Of course, Tiger didn't just play golf. He had to go to school, too. His mother says that it wasn't hard to get Tiger to do his homework. That was because he wasn't allowed to play golf until his homework was finished.

He practiced so much and worried so much about his scores that his father began to think that maybe Tiger was working too hard and was not having fun. "Quit worrying about the numbers and just have fun," Earl told his son.

"But, Daddy," nine-year-old Tlger said, "that's how I have fun—shooting low numbers!"

Tiger's dad understood. "That's okay,

Tiger Woods in Cypress, California, 1989.

son," he said. "I promise I'll never be on your case about that again."

In some ways the golf courses where Tiger played were alike, but in other ways they were very different from one another. They each had a certain number of **holes**— usually nine or eighteen—places where the golfer has to hit the ball into a **cup** in order to finish that part of the game. Each hole is laid out a little bit differently from the others. The people who design the golf courses don't want the game to be too easy, so sometimes they put lakes or trees or **sand traps** right where a ball is apt to land. The designers figure out exactly how many strokes it should take—if the golfer doesn't make any mistakes, (like hitting the ball into a pond or up in a tree)—to finish playing each hole, successfully landing the ball in the cup. The cup is always on a grassy surface called the **green**. The number of **strokes**, or shots, it should take to complete playing a hole is called **par**. To play **under par** is good; that means the player completed the hole with fewer strokes than the designer indicated.

Now that Tiger's father knew that his son really enjoyed "shooting low numbers," he began to make up special pars just for Tiger. These weren't quite as low as the par numbers the course designers had made up. After all, Tiger was still only nine years old. But Mr. Woods figured out the lowest possible number of strokes it would take to reach the green if every shot were perfect. Then he added a couple of **putts**, or short strokes. On a par four, for instance, Tiger's par might be six. If he'd made it any lower, Mr. Woods thought that maybe Tiger would feel that "he couldn't compete." Mr. Woods says, "It'd be totally unrealistic, and I'd be a stupid parent!"

One of the problems Tiger had to face when he was still very young was the fact that sometimes—when he hit a bad shot—he'd get angry and bang his club on the ground. Neither of his parents liked that kind of behavior. Even when Tiger was a little toddler watching tennis games on TV,

Enjoying a game in 1990, Tiger lines up a putt.

whenever John McEnroe or Jimmy Connors threw a tennis racquet in anger, Tida would tell him, "I will spank you in a minute if you act like that. I don't want you to ruin my reputation as a parent!"

Later, whenever Tiger slammed down his club after a bad shot, his dad would ask, "Who's responsible for that bad shot?"

And Tiger would answer sadly, "I am."

Tiger really tried to control his temper, but too often he'd take out his anger on his club, slamming it to the ground. When his parents questioned him about it, he'd answer "I don't want to do it. It just happens. I'm trying very hard."

"I know you're trying," his dad told him.

"Just keep trying. As you grow and mature, you can turn this into an advantage."

Then one day Tiger reported to his father, "Dad, I wanted to bang my club today, but I said, 'No. I'm just going to hit the ball real solid!'"

"And that's how he learned to play angry," says Earl Woods about his famous son today. "Because we allowed him space, then made him take responsibility for his actions."

Another important thing happened to Tiger when he was nine. He got to go to Thailand, his mother's native country. There he met some of his aunts, uncles, and cousins and got a close-up look at the interesting land where his mother grew up.

"In many ways," he says, "I consider Thailand 'home.'"

Tida Woods says, "Tiger has Thai, African, Chinese, American Indian, and European blood. He can hold everyone together!"

One spring day when Tiger was eleven years old, he spent a whole afternoon in his room working with posterboard, scissors, paste, and markers. He was making a special chart to hang up over his bed. He divided the poster board into three columns. Down the left-hand column, he carefully wrote the names of all of the most important golf tournaments. At the top of the middle column,

Tiger Woods and his parents in 1990.

he pasted a picture of golf star Jack Nicklaus that he'd found in a magazine. Nicklaus had just won the Masters Golf Tournament, the game's most important event, for the sixth time! No one else in the world had ever done that. Below the picture, young Tiger wrote in Nicklaus's age at the time he had won each tournament.

At the top of the third column, he neatly lettered *TIGER WOODS*. "I wanted to be the youngest player ever to win the majors," Tiger admits, smiling. "Jack Nicklaus was my hero. I thought it would be great to accomplish all the things he did even earlier than he accomplished them!"

It wasn't too long before Tiger was able

to begin filling in the spaces under his name on that chart. By the time he was twelve, he had gone undefeated in nearly thirty Southern California junior golf tournaments—and most of them had more than one hundred young players competing!

By the time Tiger entered his teens, he had played golf with some of the world's most famous players. He had played with Sam Snead. Lee Trevino had presented him with one of his trophies. Such well-known golfers as Greg Norman, John Daly, and even Jack Nicklaus had played with the remarkable young black man who had become the United States Junior Amateur Champion and the holder of a record six junior world titles!

At the Riviera Country Club in Los Angeles, California, high school sophomore Tiger Woods—aged sixteen years and two months—became the youngest golfer ever to play in a PGA (Professional Golf Association) Tour event, the 1992 L.A. Open. By this time, Tiger was 6'1" tall and weighed 140 pounds. He played well, even though he made some mistakes. "I've got a lot of growing to do," Tiger told a reporter that day, "both physically and mentally. But I'll play these guys again—eventually."

Tiger's dad knew that Tiger would have to be really tough mentally if he was going to play against the professional golfers. He knew about some of the things that might

Tiger at the L. A. Open in 1992 with his gallery behind him.

distract a golfer, so he set out to teach Tiger
how to play his best—no matter what else
was happening around him. Earl Woods did
distracting things on purpose while Tiger
tried to concentrate on his game. Mr. Woods
would suddenly jingle the change in his
pocket or would roll a golf ball in front of
Tiger. He made the brakes of the golf cart
squeak or dropped a golf bag full of clubs.
For two whole years he tested Tiger's nerves
this way, promising that all the young man
had to do to make him stop was to say,
"That's enough!"

But Tiger never said it. And when Earl
Woods was sure that his son had learned the
lesson completely, he told him, "I promise

you, as long as you live—you'll never meet any person as mentally tough as you."

Tiger was beginning to attract some extra attention wherever he played. As United States Junior Amateur champion, Tiger found that he had some fans following him around on the course. They'd shout, "You the kid!" or they would hold up signs that read: *GO GET 'EM, TIGER!* When Tiger played his first PGA event, there was a crowd of about 3,000 people following the golfers as they played. Golfers call these people the **gallery.** There were television cameras there, too. "I've never had a gallery before," Tiger said. "I wasn't used to it. Even when I hit a bad shot, people clapped!"

By the time Tiger was seventeen and a junior in high school, he'd won the U.S. Junior Amateur competition three times. No one had done that before. And no black golfer had ever won the championship. But Tiger was starting to get used to "firsts."

The following August, Tiger made golf history again, becoming the youngest winner of America's oldest golf championship—the U.S. Amateur. It was his fourth try, and Tiger was "on track" to reach his goal of being the youngest player ever to win the majors. After Tiger won, he immediately found his dad in the crowd and give him a big hug. When Tiger went home after the tournament, he went up to his bedroom. He

Tiger Woods, winner of the 1996
U. S. Amateur Championship at
Pumpkin Ridge Golf Club in
Cornelius, Oregon.

took a marker from his desk. Next to the line that read "U.S. Amateur," he carefully printed his age: 18 years, 8 months. He'd beaten Jack Nicklaus by one month!

In September, Tiger entered Stanford University. He studied business, and—of course—signed up to play on Stanford's golf team. Tiger found that college golf and college studies took up almost all of his time. He didn't feel that he was doing his best, even though he had a *B* average in his studies and was named as an All-American first-team golfer.

By this time the name "Tiger Woods" was recognized all over the world. Tiger had been invited to play in the Scottish Open and the British Open. He'd be playing against some of the finest golfers in the world—players like Greg Norman, Nick Faldo, and Fred Couples. He asked his Stanford coach, Butch Harmon, "Butch, how far away am I? When will I be that good?"

"You just have to keep working," the coach told him. "You've got so much to learn."

When Tiger played in the 1996 NCAA (National Collegiate Athletic Association) golf championship tournament, an attendance record was set. *Sports Illustrated* reported, "Of the 14,694 tickets purchased, roughly 14,000 were bought by people who came to see if Tiger Woods of Stanford really

Representing Stanford at the 1996 NCAA Division I Men's Golf Championship, Tiger Woods brought home first-place honors.

is the best amateur golfer to stroll down a fairway since . . . Nicklaus was at Ohio State."

It was a four-day event, and nineteen-year-old Tiger started well. He took the lead on the first day, broke a course record on the second day, and on the third day headed into the final round with a nine-shot lead. Someone asked if it was "easy out there."

"No." said Tiger. "There's still one more day. Anything can happen."

Things didn't go well at all for Tiger on that last day. One shot went into a lake. Another flew into the gallery. Still, he won with a four-point margin, even though this wasn't quite the way he wanted to win his first NCAA title. Tiger wanted to be the best collegiate golfer in America. At the same time, he wanted to do well in his studies. He worked hard at both. After he took his final exams at the end of his second year at Stanford, he went home to Cypress, California. He spent most of his time that summer with his childhood friends, just hanging out, riding his bike, and playing Nintendo. (Tiger likes the Nintendo combat games best.) Of course, he also worked on his game. And thought about his future.

Tiger had an important decision to make. Should he finish his college education at Stanford or was he ready now to become a professional golfer? He asked several people what they thought. He asked some famous

golfers he'd met among the touring pros. He
talked to Greg Norman and Curtis Strange.
He talked to Fred Couples and Ernie Els.
Should he accept an endorsement deal with
Nike (clothes and shoes) and Titleist (golf
balls and clubs), which could add up to $60
million over the next five years? Was he
actually ready to be a professional at the
age of twenty? The pros he talked to all told
him they believed that he was ready—both
physically and mentally—for the 1997 PGA
Tour.

Tiger decided to go for it. He promised
his parents that someday he'd return to college to complete his education. Meanwhile,
he had a lot of work ahead of him. Coach

Butch Harmon worried about the young golfer. "All the amateur titles Tiger has won won't mean anything," he said. "He'll have to prove himself in a hard environment where there is no mercy. He's going to have to grow up faster than I'd like him to."

Tiger had a big challenge ahead of him. In order to qualify for the 1997 PGA Tour, he had to become one of the top 125 money-winning players in the world. And he had only two months in which to do it!

Tiger figured out that he needed to win about $150,000. That meant he had to either win or come in second in a major tournament, or else finish within the top ten in several of them. Tiger was taller now, and heavier. He'd grown to 6'2" tall, and he weighed 155 pounds. He decided to play in the next six scheduled PGA tournaments. He tied for sixtieth place on his first try. Not good enough. He tried harder—and improved every week. He came in eleventh on his second try. Then fifth. Then third. Then first.

After his fifth professional tournament, Tiger Woods was already fortieth on the money list—with $437,194 in prize money— and he had an invitation to the 1997 Masters Tournament, America's most important golf- ing competition.

The Masters Tournament is always played in the same place—the Augusta National Golf

Club in Augusta, Georgia, where the first Masters was held in 1934. Actually, Tiger had already played on the difficult, beautiful course twice—when he was U.S. Amateur champion. But this was to be his first appearance at Augusta as a professional.

Tiger prepared carefully. When he'd played there before, he'd still been a student at Stanford. There'd been final exams and papers to write and grades to worry about. This time he had nothing on his mind except golf. He did some research and found films and videos of previous tournaments. He studied the way others had played the different holes. He knew that Augusta was going to be a good course for the way he liked to play—with plenty of long, high shots. "I worked very hard on my game in general," Tiger said. "I spent time away from everybody where I could focus one-hundred percent on my practice."

Tiger knew that top golfers like Arnold Palmer, Gary Player, and even Jack Nicklaus had each played in the Masters at least four times before winning. Did Tiger actually think he had a chance to win the Masters on his first try? "I think so," Tiger said. "It can happen."

The first day of the four-day tournament started badly for Tiger. He had a couple of wild tee shots. He seemed headed for high numbers by the time he had completed the ninth hole. But then, on the tenth, he hit a good, solid drive. He finished that hole with a score of one under par, which is called a **birdie** in golf language. Tiger started to feel better. He did the same thing on the twelfth hole. And the thirteeneth. On the fifteenth hole, he did even better. He scored two under par, which is called an **eagle**. Another birdie at the seventeenth and Tiger's name was among those at the top of the **leader board**, the list of the players with the best scores in a tournament.

On the second day at Augusta, Tiger took control. By the end of the day, he was in the lead. This was what he'd planned. "This is what I came here to do," he told reporters.

"To try and win the tournament."

But the championship was only halfway over. Tiger knew he needed to do a really good job on the third day. When the gallery was empty and all the reporters, photographers, and the other golfers had left, Tiger was all alone on the driving range, still practicing. "I can always get better," he said.

He was right. He did get better! Tiger went into the last day of the tournament with a nine-shot lead over his closest challenger. It was the largest lead at that point in the tournament's sixty-one-year history!

But things can change quickly at the Masters, and Tiger knew he couldn't relax— even though almost everyone was confident

Tiger celebrates on the 18th hole after winning the 1997 Masters Tournament in Augusta, Georgia.

that he'd win. Tiger was confident, too. He planned to wear a red shirt—something he always does on the last day of a competition that he expects to win. The night before the final day, Tiger's dad told him, "Son, this will probably be one of the toughest rounds you've ever had to play in your life. If you go out there and be yourself, it will be one of the most rewarding rounds you've ever played."

Earl Woods was right. Tiger not only won the Masters that day, earning the right to wear the special green jacket that always is given to the Masters champion, but he did it in record-setting style. He became the youngest winner. He became the first African-American winner. He had the widest margin of victory.

He broke six course records for low scores. After he was sure he'd won, he did the same thing he'd done after winning the U.S. Amateur tournament. He found his parents in the crowd and gave them each a big hug!

Tiger knew there'd be other big championship games in his future: the British Open, the PGA Championship, and the Ryder Cup matches between Europe and America. But being the youngest person to ever win the Masters was special. Tiger was really happy when he realized that so many kids are interested in golf because of him. "I think that now kids will think golf is cool," he said after his big win. "And I think they'll start playing it!"

Tiger now has a house of his own in Orlando, Florida. It is close to a fine golf course, so he can get in plenty of practice whenever he wants to. His mom and dad still have the house where he grew up in Cypress, California. He still loves to go home to visit, to keep in touch with his old friends—and if that big piece of posterboard still hangs over the bed in his old room—to continue to fill in the spaces under the name TIGER WOODS with still more firsts!

Masters Champion Tiger Woods has plenty to smile about.

ace–also called a "hole-in-one."

ball–a golf ball has a dimpled surface and is approximately 1 1/2 inches in diameter and weighs approximately 1 1/2 ounces.

birdie–one stroke less than par for a hole.

bogey–one stroke more than par for a hole.

cup–the hole on the putting green where the player tries to make the ball go.

drive–the long, first hit of each hole in a game of golf.

driving range–a place where people practice hitting a golf ball off a tee. Typically, the person "rents" a bucket full of golf balls and hits each one of them, trying to improve both the length of the drive as well as the accuracy of each drive.

eagle–two strokes less than par for a hole.

gallery–the spectators at a golf tournament.

green–the smooth, grassy surface that surrounds the hole, or cup. Also known as the "putting green."

hole–also called the cup, is on the green and is the place where the golfer is trying to make the golf ball land. The cup is 4 1/2 inches in diameter. Also, the total playing area from the tee to the cup is referred to as a hole—a golf course has eighteen holes, each one specially designed to be different.

leader board–the list of players with the best scores in the tournament, listed in order from best to next best, and so on.

par–the number of strokes that course officials have decided a player should use to place the ball into the cup. For instance, a hole that is a "par four" is one in which it should take a player four strokes to place the ball into the cup. Under par is good; it means that it took fewer strokes than the set number to put the ball into the cup. Over par means that it took the player more than the set number of strokes to put the ball into the cup.

putt–a soft hit that takes place on the green using a putter. It is usually the stroke that lands the ball into the cup.

sand traps–mounded areas on certain holes of a golf course that are filled with sand. They are near the green or along the fairway and are there to increase the difficulty of playing the particular hole.

stroke–a hit or attempted hit of the golf ball. Each swing counts, whether the ball is hit or not.

tee–a wooden or plastic peg that holds the ball up off the ground so the player can drive the ball better.

teeing off–to start play on a particular hole; another name for a drive. The ball is hit off a tee.

Front cover—*1995 U.S. Amateur Championship*
Photo Copyright © 1997 ALLSPORT USA
J.D. CUBAN. ALL RIGHTS RESERVED.

Back cover—Photo Copyright © 1997
THE ST. PETERSBURG TIMES, St. Petersburg, Florida.

Pages 3, 30, and 31—Photos copyright © 1997 ALLSPORT USA
PATRICK MURPHY-RACEY. ALL RIGHTS RESERVED.

Pages 11 and 15—Photos copyright © 1997 ALLSPORT USA
ALAN LEVENSON. ALL RIGHTS RESERVED.

Page 19—Photo copyright © 1997 ALLSPORT USA
KEVIN LEVINE. ALL RIGHTS RESERVED.

Page 23—Photo copyright © 1997 ALLSPORT USA
CARY NEWKIRK. ALL RIGHTS RESERVED.

Page 27—Photo copyright © 1997 ALLSPORT USA
J.D. CUBAN. ALL RIGHTS RESERVED.

Pages 41 and 45—Photos copyright © 1997 ALLSPORT USA
DAVID CANNON. ALL RIGHTS RESERVED.

The making of a *World-class* Champion

Tiger Woods

written by **Carol Perry**

First printing by Worthington Press 1997.

Published by PAGES Publishing Group
801 94th Avenue North, St. Petersburg, Florida 33702

Printed in the United States of America

Cover & interior design by Michael Petty

Worthington Press®

2 4 6 8 10 9 7 5 3 1

ISBN 0-87406-885-1